Sonja Linden

Sonja is an award-winning playwright, whose plays have been produced in London and in regional theatres in the UK as well as in the United States and Australia. London productions include *Call Me Judas* (Paines Plough, Finborough Theatre), *The Jewish Daughter,* sequel to Brecht's *The Jewish Wife,* (New End Theatre) and *The Strange Passenger (*Paines Plough, Battersea Arts Centre and National Tour).

   I Have Before Me A Remarkable Document Given To Me By A Young Lady From Rwanda was written in response to her encounters with a number of young Rwandan refugees at the Medical Foundation for the Care of Victims of Torture, where she has been Writer-in-Residence since 1997. The play will receive its American premiere at the Kansas City Repertory Theatre in April 2005.

   Sonja is currently working on a commission from APT Films and BBC Films to co-write with director Sarah Gavron a feature film about a young Iranian asylum seeker.

Also by Sonja Linden

Price: £7.99
ISBN 09546912-9-6

"Scars are like medals. They show we have taken part in the life."

Inspired by the real life testimony of people who have sought refuge in the UK *Crocodile Seeking Refuge* is an incisive look at the asylum stories behind the headlines.

'Its theme could hardly be more topical, or more powerful — hope, human resilience and courage are set alongside descriptions of torture and injustice that are deeply affecting.'

THE TIMES

iceand*fire*

presents

I Have Before Me
A Remarkable Document
Given To Me By A Young Lady
From Rwanda

by

Sonja Linden

AURORA METRO PRESS

First printed in 2004 by Aurora Metro Publications Ltd.
www.aurorametro.com Tel: 020 8747 1953
I Have Before Me A Remarkable Document Given To Me By A Young Lady From Rwanda : Play and introduction ©
copyright Sonja Linden 2004
Reprinted 2005 2007
Cover design: Jimmy Turrell © copyright 2004

Trade distribution:
UK - Central Books Tel: 020 8986 4854 Fax: 020 8533 5821
USA - Theatre Communications Group, N.Y. Tel: 212 609 5900
Canada - Playwrights Union of Canada Tel: 416 703 0013

ISBN 978-09546912-3-7
Printed and bound by CPI Antony Rowe, Eastbourne

To Lea Chantal

whose remarkable story and indomitable spirit
inspired this play

iceand*fire*

We passionately believe art has a role to play in communicating one of the most pressing issues of today – the growing displacement of peoples from conflict zones. In a world increasingly overshadowed by international tensions, we aim to present to British audiences stories of individuals whose lives have been touched by these events.

The company was founded in January 2003 by Sonja Linden, playwright and Writer-in-residence at the Medical Foundation for the Care of Victims of Torture. Here she set up the Write to Life Project, a creative and testimonial writing programme offering clients of the Foundation the opportunity to discharge their painful experiences of persecution and exile through the act of writing. Inspired by her seven year residency at the Medical Foundation, Sonja Linden is concerned to represent refugees as "ordinary people caught up in extraordinary circumstances." (Eli Wiesel, *Holocaust survivor, writer, Nobel laureate)*.

The company's launch production *I Have Before Me A Remarkable Document Given To Me By A Young Lady From Rwanda* was first produced at the Burton-Taylor Studio Theatre, Oxford in July 2002 for one week as part of Oxford Africa Week. The play's London premiere, a four week run in June 2003 at the Finborough Theatre, marked the launch of iceand*fire*. This production received considerable critical acclaim and was subsequently produced by Theatre Works at the 2003 Edinburgh Festival, and by BBC Radio World Service Drama.

In 2004, the Arts Council England awarded the company funding to tour the play to 30 venues across the UK in autumn 2004, to coincide with the tenth anniversary of the Rwanda genocide.

The company's second production, *Crocodile Seeking Refuge* is currently in development for a London run in 2005.

Artistic Director — Sonja Linden
Producer — Sarah Sansom
Patrons — Oona King MP, Juliet Stevenson, Arnold Wesker
Directors — Jane Dorner (chair), Moris Farhi (MBE), Katherine Klinger, Malcolm Smart, Matthew Reisz, Alexis Rwabizambuga.

iceand*fire*
75 Hillfield Park
London N10 3QU
Tel:0207 482 4255 / 0208 444 5228
Fax: 0208 444 2322
E-Mail:info@iceandfire.co.uk

The company is supported by the Indigo Trust and Arts Council England. ice**and**fire is a company limited by guarantee. Registered in England No 4648400 Charity 1062174

Biographies

Drew Ackroyd — Director

Drew trained at Rose Bruford College. Recent directing credits include the London Premiere of *I Have Before Me*...., the European Premiere of Larry Kramer's *The Destiny of Me* (Finborough Theatre), *Ciboulette* (San Francisco Opera Studio), *Fish Tales* (National Tour), *No Time To Cry* (MTV). Rehearsed Readings include *Castro's Beard* (The Arts Theatre), *A Minor Dark Age* (The Actors' Centre), *The Modern Man* (Producers Club NYC). Assistant Directing credits include *Natural Inclinations* (Finborough Theatre), *Barber of Seville* (European Chamber Opera National Tour) and *Dark of the Moon* (Westminster Theatre). He studied Forum Theatre and the methodology of Augusto Boal with the Centre for the Theatre of the Oppressed, Physical Story Telling with Clive Mendus of Theatre de Complicite and Contact Improvisation with Rick Zoltowsky. Drew also teaches, is a freelance script reader for BBC Radio Four, Co Artistic Director of Productions Absolute and an Associate Director at the Caird Company.

Mishi L. Bekesi — Asst Company Stage Manager

Mishi (aka Deeperred) is a sound designer; sound engineer; DJ and stage manager. He works extensively on the International and London theatre, music, fashion and club scenes. His recent works include: technical manager of several projects for Steve Frost; Boothby Graffoe comedy; Antonio Forcione music; Linda Marlowe theatre; Fresco Theatre 2003 tour and Prince O' Neill productions.

Rebecca Clatworthy – Deputy Stage Manager

Becky is in her final year at the Central School of Speech and Drama, where she is studying for a BA in stage management. She has worked on numerous productions within college including, *The Storm*, *Rape upon Rape*, *As You Like It*, and most recently *The Quest* at the Minack Theatre, Cornwall. Outside of college Becky has worked on a new musical *The Biz*, *Now That's Musicals....* with Cygneture Productions and this year's festival for new writing at the Polka theatre, Wimbledon. Her television work includes *Record of the Year* 2002 and *Basil Brush*.

Atlanta Duffy – Designer

Atlanta trained at Motley Theatre Design School and the Lyric Theatre, Hammersmith. She has designed for Theatre, Opera and Dance for: Bristol Old Vic, Lyric Theatre, Hammersmith, West Yorkshire Playhouse, Tricycle Theatre, Southwark Playhouse, RADA, Arcola Theatre, BAC, Stephen Joseph Theatre, Birmingham Rep and Oxford Playhouse. Recent work includes *Come Out Eli* – Time Out Award Winner, *The Way of the World* – Dir. Selina Cadell, Wilton's Music Hall, *Trojan Women* – Dir. Deborah Paige, RADA, Masquerade Costumes for *Waingi* – Dir. Peter Badejo, Greenwich & Docklands Festival, *Women of Owu* – Collective Artistes Tour, and *Death and the Maiden* – Dir. Chuck Mike, Lagos, Nigeria.

Suzann McLean – Juliette

Suzann trained at the Italia Conti Academy and has worked extensively in theatre; credits include Isabella in *Measure for Measure* (RNT), *Sense of Belonging* (Manchester), *Angie Baby* (Young Vic), *Trojan Women*, (Chipping Norton) *Romeo and Juliet*, (Keswick), *Equianano*, (National Tour), *The Magic Box*, (Tricycle Theatre), *Vengeance*, (Hackney Empire), *Ozulumba*,

(Bloomsbury Theatre), *Jack & The Beanstalk* (Theatre Royal, Stratford East), *Little Shop of Horrors,* (Ipswich), *Blue Girl* (Vienna's English Theatre) and the critically acclaimed national tour of *Bonded* (Tiata Fahodzi). Suzann recently shot a medical video to help those with Sickle Cell Anaemia. She has also appeared in various commercial, television and audio productions including *Casualty, Face at the Window, Coupling, The A-Force, Baby Father* (audio) and *Grange Hill* (all for the BBC). Film credits include *To Strike A Chord,* (Central TV), *Coco Dance (*Slim Chance Productions*) Jesus Christ Superstar,* (video) and the female lead in *White Light* for UIPL, an independent film based on a modern day Jesus Christ, to be released this year.

Gabrielle Moss — Education Consultant

Gabrielle undertook post-graduate studies in Arts in the Community at the Liverpool Institute for Performing Arts (LIPA) after which she spent two years as Education Director of Besht Tellers Theatre Company . Gabrielle has acted as Education Consultant for Northwood Holocaust Education Project — developing and delivering a unique Holocaust education programme for secondary school students, including teaching about Rwandan genocide as a key component; The Red Room — researching, compiling and designing an Education Pack to accompany the company's production *Animal;* and *IDworks!* — developing and trialling a Key Stage 1 Emotional Literacy curriculum. Gabrielle has worked with, amongst others, Hampstead Theatre; The Bull Theatre, Barnet; Half Moon Young People's Theatre; and Children's Discovery Centre *Discover*, Stratford, London. In 2003, Gabrielle established Polygon Arts, a community and educational organisation which exists to encourage Active Citizenship through drama and music, for which she is a Director. Gabrielle is currently studying for her MA in Drama and

Theatre in Education at the Central School of Speech and Drama.

Sophie Nathan – Assistant Designer

Sophie studied English and Philosophy at Leeds University, after which she spent three years managing events, including a year as Events Officer for Leeds University, and Marketing Manager for the Islington International Festival. On completing a Foundation Course in Art and Design at Westminster and Kingsway College, Sophie spent a year at the Arcola Theatre in Hackney assisting designers, constructing, scenic painting, mask and prop making. Sophie was the production manager on a new writing piece, *Owner/ Occupier* and set and costume designer for a devised piece called *Out of Man*. Sophie graduated this year from the Theatre Design Course at Motley.

Sarah Sansom — Producer

Sarah has been with Ice and Fire since November 2003. Previous work includes producing for: Arcola Theatre, Dance United, Theatre and Beyond, Pillion Productions and The Non-Violence Foundation, plus managing, marketing and tour booking for Union Dance. Directing credits include: *Pass the Parcel* (London Talent, Theatre Royal Stratford-East), *Fair Ground* (Cardboard Citizens forum theatre piece, Polka Theatre and schools tour), *A Woman's Place* devised by women refugees (The Albany, Hoxton Hall, Oxford House, London and the British Council *Sense of Place Festival*), *Shout* (Arcola Theatre), *Time Won't Wait* (Old Market Theatre, Brighton International Festival), *Target* (Festival for Women in the Performing Arts, Hanover Expo 2000). Other theatre work delivered for refugees and asylum seekers has been with Refugee Women's Association, Praxis Refugee Centre, Albanian Youth Action and Company of Angels.

Catriona Silver — Lighting Designer

Catriona has worked previously with Atlanta Duffy on the national tour of Femi Osofisan's *Women of Owu*— Dir. Chuck Mike. Recent work includes: *The Associate* at The National Theatre, and *Inside Out* with Clean Break Theatre Company. She lit many theatre productions while resident lighting designer at The Palace Theatre, Westcliff-on-Sea. Having completed a Masters in lighting at University College London, she has expanded her interest in lighting to encompass architectural lighting design and the physiology of vision and has developed a lighting proposal for the Trinity Buoy Wharf area of London.

Tim Speechley — Company Stage Manager

After graduating in stage management at Guildhall of Music and Drama, London, Tim went on to work in provincial rep, several West End productions and then took a seven year residency in stage management at the National Theatre. Tim is a lighting tutor at RADA and has spent the last fifteen years touring international drama and dance; worldwide companies include the Moscow Classical Ballet, the National Dance Company of Guinea and the Moscow State Circus. Tim's lighting design connections in world music include: Rachid ta Ha from Algeria, Femi Kuti and Keziah Jones from Nigeria.

Jane Watkins — Sound Designer

Jane studied at Guildhall School of Music under Malcolm Singer and Simon Bainbridge and at Dartington International Summer School under Judith Weir (Scholarship Britten Pears Trust). Recent theatre music engagements include *Pea Green Boat* (Stewart Lee/ BAC/ Traverse Edinburgh), *Valentine* (Actors Centre), *Widows* (Steven Little/ ALRA), *I Have Before Me*....(Drew

Ackroyd/Ice and Fire), *Modern Man* (New End), *The Sea* (Byre Theatre), *Singing, Dancing, Acting* (Soho Theatre), *Twelfth Night* (National Theatre Studio), *Much Ado* (Byre Theatre), *Twelfth Night* (Cambridge Arts Theatre), *Burleigh Grimes* (Bridewell Theatre), *Medea in Jerusalem* (Rattlestick Theatre, New York). Animation music for: *Crapston Villas* (assistant composer Spitting Image), *64 Zoo Lane* (assistant composer Millimage). Ballet includes *The Quest for Corolaine* (The Arden Holford Ballet School).Concert works for: The Junior String Orchestra (Royal Irish Academy of Music, Dublin), The Vent Saxophone Quartet. Published work includes *Santa Pod Velodrome* (Guildhall Examinations Service).

Joe Young – Simon

Joe trained at the Drama Centre, London. Recent theatre includes: Jackson in *The Hired Man* (Salisbury Playhouse), Lt. Bus Adams in *South Pacific* (National Theatre), Macheath in *The Beggars Opera* (Queens, Hornchurch), Bill Sikes in *Oliver!* (Palladium), Sammy in *Blood Brothers* (Phoenix). Also in the West End, *The Importance* (Ambasadors), *Rope* (Wyndhams); Rep seasons at York, Swansea, Leatherhead, Northampton, Norwich, Nottingham; tours for Bubble Theatre as Orin the Dentist in *Little Shop of Horrors,* Henry Clerval in April de Angelis' *Frankenstein* (LATC). Joe is an Associate Artist with Theatre and Beyond, a Brighton-based new writing company. Television roles include King Ferdinand in *Christopher Columbus DNA* (Discovery), Jake in the horror series *Dark Realm* (Warner Brothers), *London's Burning, Lyttons Diary, Doctor Who* and *Live One* (Sky One).Joe is also an award-winning soundtrack composer. Recent work includes a Friday Play for Radio 4, *Full Blown*, by Anita Sullivan.

I Have Before Me A Remarkable Document Given To Me By A Young Lady From Rwanda

by

Sonja Linden

Juliette   Suzann McLean

Simon   Joe Young

Director   Drew Ackroyd
Producer   Sarah Sansom
Designer   Atlanta Duffy
Assistant Designer   Sophie Nathan
Lighting Designer   Catriona Silver
Sound Designer   Jane Watkins
Company Stage Manager   Tim Speechley
Asst Company Stage Manager Mishi Bekesi
Deputy Stage Manager   Rebecca Clatworthy
Education Consultant   Gabrielle Moss
Production Photographer   Deborah Sandersley
Graphic Designer   Jimmy Turrell

I Have Before Me A Remarkable Document Given To Me By A Young Lady From Rwanda

Shortly after I started working with clients of the Medical Foundation for the Care of Victims of Torture, I met a young woman from Rwanda, whose impulse to write had started in a refugee camp shortly after the murder of her entire family. What started out as a testimonial act, the writing out of her family's experience of genocide, became, in addition, an act of healing as a result of which she reported that she felt 'clean' and that her nightmares and headaches had ceased. For two and a half years, she had worked on this book on her own, writing in her mother tongue and wrestling day after day with her enormously painful story, often tearing up the previous day's work at 5 o' clock in the morning, when she started her daily writing. Even while she was immersed in the process of writing her book, she recognised its therapeutic value, talking about writing in order to take the pain 'away from my heart'.

The healing she achieved was done at enormous cost since it meant confronting and expressing with full force the negative emotions that overwhelmed her in the years following the genocide. So inspired was I by her story, that when I came to write something of my own, as part of my writing residency, it was infused with her spirit and her struggle to write. *I Have Before Me A Remarkable Document Given To Me By A Young Lady From Rwanda* tells the story of an uneasy relationship between Simon, a struggling British poet in his mid-forties and Juliette, a young survivor of the Rwandan genocide, who comes to him for help with her book. My challenge as a playwright was to transform this into a piece of theatre that would engage an audience. Humour, remarkably, became an important component to create a sense of balance and draw the audience in; humour largely drawn from the cultural divide between the Englishman and the young African woman. It is this aspect of the play as well as Juliette's plight and feistiness that audiences have most remarked upon.

Many people have commented on the lengthy title of my play, some thinking it brilliantly arresting, others finding it annoyingly unwieldy – 'it takes up all the answerphone tape at the Box Office', – 'it uses up too much space in the listings column', – 'it'll frighten audiences away because it has the word Rwanda in it,' are some of the criticisms I've received. Whenever I've been challenged in this way, I've been reminded of the response of another author of another work on Rwanda: Philip Gourevitch, called his book: *We wish to inform you that tomorrow we will be killed with our families*. Like my title, it was a quote from the text, but here the quote was taken from real life – the desperate cry for help from seven pastors in charge of two thousand terrified Tutsis taking shelter in a church compound. The help was not forthcoming. For Gourevitch, impatience with his title seemed symptomatic of the West's indifference to a genocide taking place in a tiny country, off the map, in faraway darkest Africa. Similarly, my long title is a deliberate challenge to our short attention span where Rwanda is concerned.

As the daughter of refugees from Nazi Germany, I have felt all the more compelled to draw attention to this appalling late chapter in twentieth century history, a chapter that has such strong parallels with the Final Solution. Tragically, as I write this, a new genocide threatens in Western Sudan, transgressing once more the idealism of the post-Holocaust slogan of 'Never Again'.

Sonja Linden

I Have Before Me
A Remarkable Document
Given To Me By A Young Lady
From Rwanda

Sonja Linden

First performed at the Burton-Taylor Theatre, Oxford, July 2002.

Characters:

Juliette   A young Rwandan woman in her twenties

Simon   A British poet in his forties

Time and Place:

1999 – five years after the Rwandan genocide. London.

Author's note:
Rwandan language is indicated by [ ]
Phonetic spelling to aid pronunciation is indicated by *
A stroke (/) marks the point of interruption in overlapping dialogue.

Prologue

Juliette *(offstage)* They came to our house in the morning. Some of them were our neighbours. The president had been killed in the night. There was a curfew. On the radio they said nobody can go out or they will be shot. My father was very worried. We all stayed together the whole night. And in the morning there was a knock at our door. We saw it was our neighbours and my father thought this is maybe good, they will help us hide. Then we saw the others, eight or nine of them, with machetes. "What's going on?" he said. Our next door neighbour, he said, "Now is the time for all the Tutsi cockroaches to die."

Scene 1

Juliette is waiting tensely in the reception area of a Refugee Centre in central London, clutching a super-market carrier bag protectively to her chest. Simon is in one of the offices at the Centre. Both are wearing casual western clothes. Simon looks a bit scruffy and Juliette very neat. They speak straight out to the audience.

Simon   Not a bad little room. Bit institutional. It's got a window at least. Not a great view. Never mind. A desk, two chairs and an empty book-case. So... wonder what she's going to be like?

Juliette   I'm early. I'm always early. I want to make a good impression. It's important. I had to take three trains to get here. I don't really mind that. I don't mind the trains. It's the tunnels I don't like when you have to change from one line to another. I get scared if I'm alone in those tunnels. Anything could happen.

Simon   My first client. An African. *(reads)* Juliette Niy... rabeza. Juliette spelled the French way. Of course, it was a French colony. Better look that up.

Juliette   I wonder what he will be like? Glasses. For sure he will wear glasses. Probably those little ones at the end of the nose. So he will look down at me like this. And he will be dressed in a smart suit, navy or black, and a white shirt and a tie. Maybe his old university tie. Oh, he must be so educated! His English will be perfect – perfect grammar, perfect spelling. I don't mind how strict he is, I need to learn. It is an opportunity for me. When he sees my book, he will see how serious I am. I will say to him, "Mr. Simon, can you help me please." And I will take it out of my bag and put it on his desk. And he will take one look and he will pick up his phone to speak to his secretary. And he will say, "Miss Smith, get me the best publisher in London please. I have before me a quite extraordinary and remarkable document given to me by a young lady from Rwanda," and he will look down his glasses at the first page and he will say to me...

Simon   Juliette ?

Scene 2
Simon's office at the Refugee Centre.

Simon *(indicating chair)* Please. Well, it's really nice to meet you, Juliette. You're my first customer. I'm really looking forward to working with you. Have you come far?
Juliette   Barking.

Simon   Barking. That *is* a long way. So... perhaps
you'd like to tell me a bit about yourself. How long
have you been here? In the UK?

Juliette   Five months.

Simon   And did you come here alone or...?

Juliette   Yes.

Simon   That must be difficult... to be here all
alone, new country, new language, new customs, must
be hard. The nearest I ever got to it was when I spent
a few months in India. Backpacking. Of course it
wasn't the same... naturally.

Juliette   You don't have a phone.

Simon   Er... no, no I don't, do I? *(beat)* Anyway,
you've been here five months and you live in Barking
and you've come to see me about....

Juliette   My book.

Simon   Your book! Well! May I see? Ah, it's
written in...?

Juliette   Kinyarwanda.

Simon   Kenya...?

Juliette   Kinya-rwanda. That's the language we
speak in Rwanda.

Simon   Kinya-rwanda. And what is your book
about? Is it a novel?

Juliette   It's about the genocide.

Simon   Of course. And... is it a personal account?

Juliette   It's a history of my country and what
happened in 1994 .

Simon   1994 being the year...

Juliette   ... of the genocide against the Tutsis.

Simon   I'm sorry. I didn't know the exact date.
And you were there, I mean...?

Juliette   Yes. I was there.

Simon   So... it's a... first-hand account.
Juliette   It's about what happened.
Simon   Right. And is it finished?
Juliette   Almost.
Simon   That's very impressive. It's a lot of writing.
Juliette   I did much research. I went to libraries.
Simon   Right. *(leafs through the document then hands it back)* That's quite an achievement.

Silence.

Juliette   You are a big writer...
Simon   Well...
Juliette   So you can help me to get my book published.
Simon   Ah. You want me to help you get this published. But the book isn't written in English, so...
Juliette   Someone is translating it for me.
Simon   I see. Good. I'll be able to read it then. *(beat)* Well, Juliette perhaps I should tell you a bit about what I do here at the Refugee Centre. My job here is to help people like you with their writing. Some people may want to write poetry or short pieces about what happened to them in their countries, some may want to write stories...
Juliette   How do you speak to your secretary? If you don't have a phone.
Simon   I don't actually have a secretary.
Juliette   But who types your books for you?
Simon   Well, it's mostly been poetry. And then I tend to just scribble down lines as they come to me...
Juliette   I don't understand.

Simon   Scribble, you know, dash things down.
Write things down quickly. I only type it up when I've
got the final draft of a poem.

Juliette   You type it yourself?

Simon   Oh yes, all by myself. With these two
fingers.

Juliette   I thought you were a book writer.

Simon   Well, my poetry has appeared in books.
I've had a few collections published.

Juliette   OK.

Simon   And I've got a couple of novels sitting in
the drawer.

*Juliette starts to pack away her book into the carrier
bag and stands up.*

Juliette   Thank you for your trouble.

Simon   Not at all. Are you sure there isn't
anything else I can...

Juliette   It was nice to meet you.

Simon   Well, it would be nice to meet again.
Perhaps when you've had it translated and then I
could...

Juliette   The first part will be ready next week.

Simon   Why don't you bring it to show me? Then I
could get some idea of your book. How about next
Thursday? At the same time.

Scene 3

Juliette and Simon speak straight out to the audience.

Juliette   He's no good! He can't help me. I'm not
going back there. He had a stain on his trousers. So he

can't have a wife. He must be an English bachelor. I thought he would be a proper writer. A man of letters. Not a man with a stain on his trousers. And there were no books in his room. I thought I would see rows of his books. Some in the drawer he said. Why hide them in a drawer? What was that new word.... scribble? I'll write it down. It doesn't sound too nice – scribble. He's a scribbler, that man.

Simon   Well, that was short. Sweet girl... bit naive... shy. Probably looks up to me: 'The Writer'. Well, I'll have to do something about that at our next meeting, make her more at ease. Huh! 'The Writer'!

Juliette *(opening a large manila envelope, excited as she takes out the contents)* Oh! It's so beautiful. It's typed, like a proper book. He is a good friend to do this. I didn't want to approach him because he is a Hutu but we have to believe some of them are human beings, some of them were against the killing and anyway he was here when it happened. Oh the pages are so clean! I hope it is a good translation. How will I know? I don't have any English friends. So there is only one person. The man with his books in a drawer. The scribbler.

Scene 4
Simon's office at the Refugee Centre.
Silence while Simon reads the introduction to Juliette's book.

Juliette	What do you think?
Simon	Well, I've only read a couple of pages.
Juliette	Yes?

Simon   You've packed in a lot here... the historical background, pre-colonial, colonial, post-colonial. I can see you've worked really hard.

Juliette   But is it good? That's what I need to know.

Simon   I need to read it properly. Look, could I borrow it, would that be all right, then I can read it before we meet again?

Juliette   OK.

Simon   Fine.

Juliette   I want to learn about writing.

Simon   That's great.

Juliette   Can you give me an assignment please to help me improve my writing in English.

Simon   Right... OK... let's think now... erm. Well, what about your life here in London? Do you think you could write me a piece about that. Your new life here. Where do you live? In a flat? Or, a room?

Juliette   A room. In a hostel.

Simon   Well, you could start very simply. Just write about the hostel and the people in it or even just about your room. A descriptive piece. How does that sound?

Juliette   OK.

Simon   Just write very simply, as though you were speaking to me.

Juliette   But I want to do good writing.

Simon   Some really good writers write very simply.

Juliette   Really?

Simon   Sure. Good writing is not about fancy long words. Good writing makes you see what the writer wants you to see. And feel of course. Writing is about feeling, Juliette.

Scene 5

Juliette is in her room and Simon in his 'writing hut'.

Simon   'A Description of My Room'! Jesus! I'll be asking them to write about their summer holidays next! Pathetic. And I was cock-a-hoop when I got this job, seemed like an answer to a prayer: dried-up poet and failing novelist seeks part-time work with 'writer' in job-title, to restore modicum of self-respect and income, in lieu of current occupation as house parasite with well-meaning wife acting as sole breadwinner for one year, so that struggling writer can finally complete the big novel! Yeah well it was great at the beginning, fantastic, not to have to go into work every day, just wake up, pop down to my little shed at the bottom of the garden, and have the whole day. Years and years of notes, drafts, sketches, finally to be able to put them in some sort of order. My big chance. And then...after the first hundred pages, suddenly, nothing. Everyday I think, right, today's the day I'll crack it and I sit here and ....nothing.

Juliette   'A Description of My Room'. One chair is in my room. One bed is in my room. One... wardrobe is in my room. One... The walls are grey. The ceiling is grey. The table is grey. The window is grey. The sky from the window is grey. My sweater is grey. There are no colours in my room.

A mirror is in my room. There is a face in the mirror. A girl's face. An African face. The girl looks in the mirror. She sees the face of her mother. She sees the face of her little sister. She sees the face of her grandmother. When she turns her head she sees her father's nose. She sees her uncle's chin. The girl looks in the mirror and she does nor see herself.

I must write. I must finish my book. I must. 'A Description of My Room'. I don't like this room. This room is cold. This room is dark. At night it is noisy. The girl in the next room is crazy. She is talking all the time, talking, talking like a madwoman. I feel sorry for her but I want her to go away. There is a big smell coming from her. A stinky woman's smell. I don't want her to come near me. But she always knocks on my door or she bangs on my wall. I don't like people who are so dirty.

'A Description of My Room'. I hate this room. I sit here all day and then I lie down to sleep. And it is like a prison to me because I'm frightened to go out. It is cold in this room, and lonely. I am lost in this room.

And when I look in the mirror to find myself, I see my mother, I see my little sister, I see my aunts, I see my grandmother. I see my father and my uncle. They are all there in the mirror. I see them clearly. Until they disappear. Until they are washed away. My mother's cheeks grow wet. And tears drip from my father's nose onto my uncle's chin. 'A Description of My Room'.

Scene 6
Simon's office at the Refugee Centre.

Simon	Nice to see you again, Juliette. How are you?
Juliette	Fine, thank you. And you?
Simon	Oh, not so bad. *(Pause)*

Juliette   Did you read my book?

Simon   Absolutely. We'll talk about it. But first, let's have a look at the homework.

Juliette   I didn't bring it.

Simon   Oh. Any particular reason?

Juliette   I left it on the bus.

Simon   Dog didn't eat it then?

Julicttc   Why you say that?

Simon   Just a silly schoolboy excuse, you know: "Sorry teacher, couldn't bring my homework, I left it on the bus." or "Sorry sir, the dog ate it."

Juliette   Why you talk to me about dogs?

Simon   Just teasing. I don't suppose you have a thing about dogs like we do over here. The British love their dogs! Anyway...

Juliette   We used to have dogs, Simon, many, many.

Simon   What happened to them?

Juliette   They were all killed.

Simon   Why?

Julielle   There were dead bodies everywhere and the dogs were eating them. Even the UN soldiers started to shoot them in the end. And they were good. One shot and *pow!* We knew they had these excellent weapons, but we didn't think we would ever see them use them. They didn't use them once to stop us being murdered. They just stood and they watched. Those were their orders. Only afterwards, they used them to shoot dogs, to stop them eating our dead.

Simon   I'm sorry. That's awful. And listen don't worry about the homework, it really doesn't matter. It was a stupid idea anyway.

Juliette   Homework is not stupid! Homework is important. Students must do their homework or they will not improve. If it doesn't matter, why do teachers give their students homework? Education is very important.

Simon   You're right, of course you're right. I didn't mean it wasn't important. Anyway, perhaps we should talk about your book.

Juliette   Yes. Please say to me what you think. Is it good?

Simon   Well, yes, it, it's very thorough, quite remarkably so, but... but the truth is, I think the way you've written it, it's going to be quite hard to find a publisher. I'm really sorry, because I know how important this book must be to you. But what I want to say to you Juliette is, I think we can do something about that.

Juliette   What?

Simon   Look, what you've written, there's nothing actually wrong with it, it's detailed, shocking of course, terribly shocking, awful — lists, dates, facts.... As a document of what happened it's very factual, but...it's dry, there are no feelings there, it's impersonal, there's no suggestion that it's actually been written by a survivor. *(Pause)* You are a survivor, aren't you?

Juliette   Yes.

Simon   I just wondered, I just thought you might try telling me some of the things you felt, some of *your* experiences. I thought perhaps I could help you write a different sort of book, a much more powerful book, a book that would have a lot more impact than this. The truth is, it's the personal story that will make people really understand what went on, that's what will make it real for us. And that's what will interest a publisher.

(Silence)

I mean Juliette, where is your story in all this? Can you tell me?

Juliette   No.

Scene 7

Simon is in his 'writing hut,' organising a small collection of books into a pile. The books have got bits of paper stuck in them to mark some of the pages.

Simon   OK. So that's three from *'Half a Life'*, four from, *'Griffin of the Night'*. *'The End of the Circle'*? Oh well, why not? *'Providence'* always goes down well, so does *'Bearhug'*. OK. God, I'd better get going. Bloody hell, Barking! So, am I going to call in on Juliette, or not? She didn't turn up for our next appointment, she hasn't answered my calls. I think I might have pushed her too hard. My fault. Stupid! Or should I just let it go? I mean it's up to her if she wants to come and see me. No. I can't just leave it like that. It's got to be better than giving up on her. And let's face it, they don't have a poetry festival in Barking every week.

Scene 8

Juliette's room.

Simon   I was just in your area and as, well, as I haven't been able to get hold of you by phone I... I just wanted to have word with you. Took a chance you'd be in. Hope it's OK. Hope I'm not disturbing you.

Juliette   No, really, it's OK. Please.
(Aside) What is he doing here! I am so embarrassed. I didn't get dressed properly today and my hair is not

done. Why has he come? To scold me because I didn't go and see him again? He must be very angry with me.

Simon   So, this is your room?

Juliette   Yes.

Simon *(handing her a giant bar of chocolate)* Thought you might like this.

Juliette   Thank you.

Simon *(Aside)* It's not *that* bad in here, just so bare. Apart from that poster. Mind you, who knows what her own home was like, back in Rwanda. Could have been equally spartan. *(Pause)* Who's that?

Juliette   *Boyzone!* Very popular in Rwanda.

Simon   Really? *(crosses over to the window)*

Juliette *(Aside)* What would my mother do? She would say, "Welcome, please make yourself at home." And she would invite him into the salon and offer him a seat on the leather sofa by the window. *(To Simon)* Please, sit down.

(Aside) And he would look out at the garden. And then my father would come home from the hospital and he would say, "Ah, we have a guest. We must give him whisky," and my father would laugh with his very deep laugh and say "Welcome to our house Simon". *(To Simon, formal)* Welcome to my room Simon.

Simon   Thank you. It's very... You can see Canary Wharf from here.

Juliette   I don't know.

Simon   Look, that tall building, with the flashing light.

Juliette *(strains to see it)* Oh.

Simon   Tallest building in London. Have you been there? Have you seen much of London?

Juliette   No, no, no.

Simon   Do you go out much?

Juliette   To the shops, to the library but most of the time I just stay in my room. But I have no TV, no radio, no books, nothing, nothing to do. But anyway I don't have no money to go anywhere. They don't give me money.

Simon   But you have food?

Juliette   I can buy from *Sainsburys*. With the vouchers.

Simon   I don't know how you manage without money.

Juliette   The telephone is like a big thing for me.

Simon   So what do you do if you want to make a telephone call?

Juliette   Sometimes the Refugee Centre gives me ten pounds or five pounds and then I can buy a phone card. They are very good to me. They give me soap and toothpaste because I cannot get this with the vouchers, only food.

Simon   You don't have any money at all?

Juliette   No, no, no.

Simon   So how do you get about?

Juliette   Sorry?

Simon   Travel — in London?

Juliette   I must go to the one-stop shop. They give you travel cards.

Simon   Is it far from here?

Juliette   I have to take a bus and a train.

Simon   So, they give you cards for a whole week in advance.

Juliette   No, no, no. You go there, they ask you where you want to go and they give you one travel card.

Simon   Just for that day?

Juliette   Yes.

Simon   But you need to travel to get to the travel shop. How do you pay for that?

Juliette   That's why I don't go there. Or sometimes someone gives me money, the manager of the hostel. Or I walk there. Like when I have an appointment to see you.

Simon   God!

Juliette   Now he's looking at me with eyes full of pity. I hate that! I should not have told him these things. We Tutsis are proud, we don't want nobody to know if we have problems. If we have no food to eat, we cannot show this to the neighbours. We put a big cooking pot on the stove, so people think we have to eat. Even we fill it just with water so people shouldn't know we have nothing. We don't want nobody to feel sorry for us.

Simon   So this is where you write, under the window?

Juliette   Yes.

Simon   Listen, I just came to say, sorry, sorry I pushed you about writing your book differently. I...it was insensitive of me. I'm sorry. Really. That's all I wanted to say. And please, if you still think I can help you.

Juliette   You are a teacher. I need to learn from you.

Simon   Well, I'll try. Let's talk more about what you want to write next week and about your book. When you come to the Centre. *(Pause)* I'd better be off now. Actually, I'm on my way to a poetry reading. I've been invited to read some of my poetry. Somewhere not far from here. That's why I'm in your area. You wouldn't like to come, would you?

Juliette   With you?

Simon   Yes, with me.
Juliette   Thank you.
Simon   Great.
          *(Aside)*Why did I do that? I just came to see if she was
          all right, to apologise.
Juliette *(Aside)* Why did I do that? I am so embarrassed
          to go somewhere with him. And why did he ask me?
          He feels sorry for me. But can I tell him, no? I cannot.
Simon   Do you need to eat before we go, we might
          be a while, have you had supper?
Juliette   I don't eat.
Simon   Why? You can cook here, can't you?
          There's a kitchen you can use.
Juliette   But I don't use it.
Simon   Why not?
Juliette   I told you, I don't eat. I can't. And I don't
          sleep. I only sleep like two hours or three hours a
          night, because every night, every night I'm crying.
          But you know if I want to try and make myself sleep I
          just imagine...
Simon   What?
Juliette   Is nothing. I'll get ready.

Scene 9
*Simon's car. Juliette and Simon speak straight out to the
audience.*

Simon   We could have walked there really, it isn't
          far, only a few streets away, but then I thought, maybe
          it's nice for her to be in a car for once. A bit of luxury.

Juliette   His car is old. Not like my papa's. He
    cannot be rich, Simon.

Simon   I'll put in a cassette.

Juliette   He doesn't have a CD player!

Simon   It isn't *Boyzone*.

A blast of baroque choral singing.

Juliette   It sounds like angels singing.

Simon   She hasn't said anything.

Juliette   So beautiful!

Simon   I wonder what she's thinking. Fuddy
    duddy music perhaps.

Juliette *(with eyes closed)* Angels!

Simon   Should I switch over to Radio One? No,
    leave it.

Juliette   Angels! In heaven!

Simon   I wonder what they'll make of it, at the
    reading, me turning up with a beautiful African
    princess on my arm. She *is* beautiful. Why hadn't I
    realised before what a beautiful girl she is?

Juliette   The angels have stopped singing. The car has stopped. Where are we? It looks like a pub. I don't know why we have stopped here. Oh, we are going inside. I am following Simon, up stairs, more stairs, and more stairs.

Simon   Well, well, I was wrong! Quite a /crowd.

Juliette   What a big room and so many / people.

Simon   There must be eighty to a hundred people / here.

Juliette   Simon must be/ famous!

Simon   And not just the socks and sandals brigade, young people, a lot of them / black.

Juliette   Black people, white people, brown people, all in the same room, all talking, talking, talking. Now a lady is speaking to everyone. She is quite old with very, very short hair sticking up and a ring in her nose.

Simon   Ah! I'm on with Zachary, local boy made good, that explains it — they've turned out for him.

Juliette   This lady is speaking so fast, it's difficult for me. What is she saying? Five collections of poetry ... on sale later... prizes for his poems — oh that's good Simon! — 'an exotic voice on the British landscape.' Oh la la!

Simon   This is excruciating. Oh Kathryn, I can see how carefully you've worked on this introduction but no one's interested — they just want Zachary, I can feel it. What's Juliette doing? / She's staring at Kathryn. Her face is completely blank. It's all going over her head! She's drifting, I'm sure.

Juliette   Now I am getting lost. It's too much. I have my dictionary in my bag, but, no, it's too quick. But I know she thinks he is a good poet, and I feel shame — of course a poet is not like a book writer, a poet is more bohemian; poets are not concerned with clean trousers and smart cars. I was wrong to think all those things about him. And now he is going to the front. And now the lady gives him a kiss, on his face! Ugh. And he kisses the air by her cheek. Good, Simon. Now he is speaking to us. / These young people are still talking, talking, talking. *(She looks back over her shoulder)* Shhh! That's better.

Simon   Good evening, everyone. I was asked to start off by saying a few words about writing poetry./ For me anyway...

Juliette   You look nice standing there. A button is missing in the middle of your shirt and I can see a little bit of your belly...

Simon   ...You don't set out to write the poem. The poem writes you...

Juliette   You wave your arms a lot.

Simon   ....a sea of pain surrounded by a white space...

Juliette   'A sea of pain'. Oh Simon, you are a big poet! You have a nice face Simon. How old you are? You look older than my papa... 'A sea of pain'. So you know something about suffering? You're reading a poem now. I like the sound. I can't understand it / but I like the music it makes, your voice.

Simon   I'm reading a love poem. I wrote it for Maggie. My voice is flagging. Juliette is writing something down. What? She's looking up now. She's smiling. Those perfect ivory teeth. She's radiating. She's listening. She likes it. She likes my poem. My voice is picking up. The room is electric. Here comes the tricky bit, the shock climax, the jagged edge, I've got them now. They didn't expect that from me. And Juliette? No longer smiling but leaning forward, looking at me!

Scene 10
Outside Juliette's hostel after Simon has walked her home.

Simon   So, what did you think of Zachary. Amazing wasn't he? The audience loved him. Fantastic performer. Didn't you think? *(Silence)* Juliette?

Juliette   I did not like him. Why, he was so angry? I
don't like that. Why they call him a poet? All he does
is shouting. Is no good. I like your poems Simon.
They make me calm. You are a real poet.

Simon   Well, thank you. I was sure you'd prefer
his sort of stuff. And he *was* funny, didn't you think,
funny about the British, in a very black sort of way, if
you know what I mean.

Juliette   Why he doesn't like Britain? So why he
stay here? This country is good. There is no war here.
People are kind.

Simon   Right, well I guess he doesn't see it like
you do. But you enjoyed it, the evening? You're
pleased you came.

Juliette   It was *so* good. Even just to go somewhere.
Even I didn't understand everything. Thank you
Simon, for inviting me. Before like, I didn't know
what it was, a poetry evening. But now I know poetry
is good. It's good you are a poet and not a book writer.

Simon   Books bring in more money.

Juliette   Money is not important. Believe me, I
know what is important in life now Simon.

Simon   Sure. *(beat)* Well I'd better be off. It's
nearly midnight. If I'm not quick I'll find a pumpkin
waiting for me when I get back to the pub.

Juliette   Why?

Simon   Like in the Cinderella story? Oh you
probably don't know it. I'll tell you another time.

Juliette   You don't have a wife, Simon?

Simon   I do, actually, yes.

Juliette   Oh. So she will think, "Where is my
husband? He must be at home with me."

Simon   Oh Maggie's not like that. She's very laid-
back. Relaxed. She'll be fast asleep, probably. You'd

better go in, you're shivering. You should have brought a jacket or something.

Juliette   I don't have a jacket.

Simon   Well it's only spring. It gets cold at night.

Juliette   I'm always cold in this country.

Simon   Mmm, smell that lilac!

Juliette   What?

Simon   There, right above your head, can you smell it?

Juliette   Mmm.

Simon   Oh well, I'll say good night. Will I see you at the Centre next Thursday then?

Juliette   Yes, Simon.

Simon   Good. *(beat)* You look very pretty Juliette, standing there under the lilac.

Juliette   Thank you.

Simon   Good night.

Juliette   Good night.

Scene 11

Simon and Juliette speak straight out to the audience.

Simon   It had been a good night.

Juliette   My first good night here in England.

Simon   Images of Juliette kept coming back to me as I drove home — her listening to me so intently, that moment when she smiled, her standing under the lilac tree. And then, suddenly, well, it was just a couple of phrases at first, then a few more. I stopped the car. The pockets of poets are never empty, my

Iraqi client had said to me at our last meeting. Mine had been for quite some time. And now here I was, frantically scrabbling for some scraps of paper to dash down the phrases that were coming to me, trying to keep up. Then I stuffed them into my jacket pocket, and headed for home, a pocket full of crumpled treasure, like old times.

Juliette   Everything is better than my first night in this country and my night in Hastings.

Simon   Maggie was still awake when I got back. She'd stayed up specially. All I wanted to do was to sift through my treasure, pan for gold — if there was any. But she really wanted to know how the reading had gone.

Juliette   When I found an agent to take me out of Rwanda. I trusted him to take me somewhere safe. I knew him slightly and so I trusted him.

Simon   Trust. It's crucial, isn't it, in a relationship. I had broken that trust a few times in the early days of our marriage but I'd put that behind me, that was understood.

Juliette   He organised everything and he came with me on the plane, escorted me out of the country, I didn't even have a passport, and all the time he was telling me that he would take me to a place for refugees. He would do everything for me when we got there. Where? I asked. I didn't even know where we were going.

Simon   I won't say we tell each other everything –
every relationship needs a few private corners. But we
tell each other what is important.

Juliette   After we arrived, a mini-cab took us from
Heathrow to Forest Gate — that's in the east part of
London.

Simon   But somehow I found myself telling
Maggie about the evening without mentioning
Juliette.

Juliette   "Juliette," he suddenly said, "Now I must
leave you because now I'm in a big hurry to go back to
the airport to catch my flight back home, so please go
to a church or look there's a mosque, go and ask
someone to help you." It was dark and everything
looked old and dirty and I was standing in the street
and shivering. I had no suitcase, no papers, no
money, nothing.

Simon   I did tell her that I'd been reading some of
the love poems, from that last cycle. She was touched.
And then suddenly she wanted to make love. Out of
the blue. It had been ages.

Juliette   I went up to one man, he was Indian.
"Please can you help me, I have nowhere to sleep. I
am coming from a war country." And he said, "What
will my wife think if I bring you home?" And I was
crying now.

Simon   And all I could see was Juliette, with her
dangly silver ear-rings and her shiny pink lips and her
perfect coppery sheen complexion, until I blinked

inside my head and made myself return to Maggie. And in that second, as I opened my eyes, I took in the bedside table, with Maggie's face cream, and her reading glasses and her pile of books for marking...

Juliette　　　And the Indian man said, "OK I'll take you back with me." And he did. He was so kind. The next day he took me to New Ham Council and the Council sent me to a place called Hastings. It is by the sea.

Simon　　　....and it all packed up. I couldn't do it, just couldn't. And so we just lay there, in the dark, side by side, not saying a word. And the evening vanished. It was pumpkin time, well and truly.

Juliette　　　They put me in this room, in a hotel place. It was very bad, the room, dirty and broken. I had no money, no food vouchers, nothing, and I knew nobody. And I thought maybe I should have stayed in Rwanda even though it was still dangerous for me.

Simon　　　The next day Maggie wanted to talk about it in bed, it was a Saturday and we were lying in. I said to her, "Honestly Mags, it's no big deal". But she thinks it's to do with me being too preoccupied with my work at the Centre. She thinks I'm depressed, weighed down by all those terrible stories. She thinks that it's getting to me and that I'm too involved.

Juliette　　　I had no one to talk to. I didn't know anyone. Outside it was rainy and cold and when I passed people in the street, they looked through me, not smiling at all, although they could see I must be a stranger. I felt so lonely in the streets. And then I would go to the sea, the big, grey English sea.....

Simon   I take them out sometimes, somewhere they might not have been to in London. Often, it's a park. They never go anywhere, too frightened, no money, no idea what's out there to see. They live in such small, anxious worlds. They just sit in their bleak little rooms waiting, – will they get refugee status, or will they be shunted back to the horror they escaped from.

Scene 12
Regent's Park.

Juliette   .... and I thought, "Let me just finish my life, yes, let me just finish it. Tonight I'm going to the sea and I'm going to die." And when I was going there, the manager saw me, and he followed me. I was just going to jump and he called out, "Hey Juliette, what are you doing?" and I said, "I was just going to have swim." "At night, with your clothes on? No, you come back and you tell me your problem." And when I did, he said, "Let me call New Ham Council, maybe they will take you back." And they did. It was much better than Hastings, Simon. I stayed there two months. Then after that, they sent me to the hostel.

Pause

Simon   You should write about that for your book.
Juliette   You think?
Simon   Absolutely. Anyway, now you're here and it's spring, and the sun is shining and the trees are in blossom, look at that one over there, covered in pink.

Juliette   Yesterday I tried to do some writing, to start again. But I only did one page.

Simon   That's OK. All writers have good days and bad days. It's normal.

Juliette   I don't have no good days Simon. All my writing days is bad. But if maybe you can teach me how to write better, then maybe....

Simon   Sure, but don't worry about that now, take a look around you – the trees, the flowers, the blue sky, the green grass, 'England's green and pleasant land' – that's what we call it. Must be very different for you.

Juliette   Rwanda is so much green, Simon, and so beautiful. Many mountains, covered in green, thousands of them. We call it the country of a thousand hills. *(beat)* But can I give you my writing now, then you can show me my mistakes?

Simon   Juliette, I brought you here to get away from all that for a bit.

Juliette   But I need my writing lesson, Simon, I need to learn so I can make my book good.

Simon   OK, OK. Well perhaps we can have a bit of a lesson here, if you want. Remember we talked about how to make writing more interesting, more vivid when you're describing people of places? Well, look over there, if you had to describe those flowers for example. Try that.

Juliette   Pinks and purples and blues and yellows, big, and small and tall and short...

Simon   Yes, but that's literal, remember what we did that time. Make it more figurative.

Juliette   They're waving...

Simon   Good.

Juliette   ... Waving in the wind, waving at me.

Simon   Good. Maybe they're trying to say something to you.

Juliette   They're saying... they're saying... they're saying, "Come on Juliette, smile, smile at us. No, don't look away. See how beautiful we are. We are beautiful and you are not, you are ugly girl with ugly things in your head."

Simon   You're not ugly, you're very beautiful. Believe me.

Juliette   I want to be back in my room, where it is grey. I fit better in that room. I'm sorry Simon.

Simon   No, I'm sorry. I had no idea, I thought the sight of the flower garden...

Juliette   It's not your fault Simon. You are kind to bring me here but...

Simon   Look, why don't we have the picnic. It's nothing much — just a couple of sandwiches and a bit of fruit — I thought you might like a mango. *(pulls out a couple of baguettes, two small cartons of juice, a couple of bananas and a mango)*.

Juliette   You buy this Simon, or your wife?

Simon   Englishmen are capable, you know.

Juliette   This mango is hard.

Simon   OK, fairly capable. *(feels the mango)* Sorry. What about Rwandan men?

Juliette   They are no good! They still want that we do everything for them. They are not modern, like over here.

Simon   You're not eating? Come on! You need to eat.

Juliette   What is inside?

Simon   Mozzarella.

Juliette *(tastes it gingerly then pulls a face)* It is funny. English food is funny for me.

Simon   It's Italian actually. This one's salami. Is
that OK?

Juliette   Is no good for me. My stomach is bad. I
can't eat this. I only eat very little. *(She tears off a bit
of the French bread.)*

Simon   Well, that can't do you any harm.

Juliette   We have this bread in Rwanda.

Simon   Go on, have a banana at least. At least
that's something you know from at home.

*Simon gives Juliette a banana and then takes one for
himself. Juliette watches mesmerised, as he starts to peel
it. She appears more and more amused, and as he takes
the first bite, she has to stifle her giggles.*

Juliette   I'm sorry. Sorry, Simon. I don't want to be
rude.

Simon   I haven't got food all over my face, have I?

Juliette   No, no, Simon. I'm sorry – in Rwanda,
only women and babies eat bananas. We think it's
funny to see a big man eating a banana.

Simon   Oh, right. Anything else funny about me?

Juliette   Yes. Hair. On your arms and maybe on
your here... *(shy, indicates his chest)* Some whites,
they have hair on their bodies. My little sister,
Dominique, would run away from them. To us, they
look like monkeys with all that hair. Sorry, Simon.
And blue eyes — we think they are really scary.
Dominique called white people, 'scary eyes.'

Simon   How old was she, Dominique?

Juliette   Three and a quarter. I spent all my spare
time with her, reading her stories, playing games.
"Come on Juliette, come into the garden, let's play
hiding games." And then my cousin, Nathalie comes

to find us and she shouts at me, "Why you don't help Maman with the washing up, you always run off to play with Dominique and we have to do your share." We're hiding behind a big bush and we make faces.... *(laughs girlishly)* And then Papa comes and he says, "Where are those two girls? Not hiding in the bushes I hope. I'll count to three and then I'll look behind that bush. One... two.... three!" And Dominique screams, she is so excited and he crashes through the bush and lifts her up high and he laughs... And we do this everyday sometimes.

Simon   He sounds great, your Dad.

Juliette   I was his favourite, you know.

Simon   You know what, in your book, why can't we hear about your family, why don't you describe them, make them come alive on the page. I think that would be rather wonderful don't you.

Pause

Juliette   I like your idea Simon.

Simon *(starting to put picnic remains in his bag, then produces from it, a lilac-coloured fleecy jacket)* Oh, I erm... I have something for you. Actually, it was my daughter's, but she doesn't wear it any more and I wondered, I mean you might not like it but I thought, as you didn't have a jacket... I mean she's very happy to give it to you, if that doesn't offend you or anything. The fact that it's second hand...

She puts it on, smiling her thanks.

Scene 13

Simon and Juliette are both in their rooms. They speak straight out to the audience.

Simon   It was the colour that made me buy it. Rachel wouldn't have been seen dead in it.

Juliette   It's five o'clock in the morning, the time I do my writing. Rachel's jacket is so warm. Now I must do my book again. The last one Simon says was no good, so yesterday, I took it outside and... and I threw it on the rubbish. So now I have to start again. I've tried to do what Simon says, write about my family. But it is no good. Last week I did not go to see Simon. I called him to say I have a headache. It is not a lie. I have a headache all the time. Even when I am sleeping.

Simon   I wonder how she's getting on. She didn't come last week. I think she's really struggling. I think of her a lot, sitting in that bleak little room, seeing no one, speaking to no one....

Juliette   Today is the most difficult day for me, for all Rwandan people. Today is the anniversary of the genocide, the day it all started. April the sixth. Today I must stay at home and pray until the night-time. Today is our memorial day.

Juliette begins to light a series of candles and places them on the floor in different parts of her room, and crosses herself. The lights dim gradually, leaving the stage candlelit and in semi darkness by the end of the scene. She speaks softly, her voice breaking from time to time with emotion.

Juliette *(lighting the first candle)* Papa, I was your
favourite. You were gentle and you always trusted
people, not like Mama. You remember when I asked
you when the UN came. "Do you think they can save
us?" and you said, "Of course, it's why they are here,"
and Mama said, "Why do you have so much faith in
them? Because they are white?" It is for you I am
writing this book to make you proud.
(lights the second candle)
You are sleeping now. You are peaceful. Mama, I
know I was a bad girl sometimes with you. We had big
fights, big fights. But I know you loved me and... I
loved you. Even though sometimes I thought I hated
you.
(lights a third candle)
Oh Alice. Oh Alice, my big, big sister. You were so
beautiful. Like Papa's sister Lucie, with those big, big
eyes. All the boys were crazy for you but you just
laughed at them.
(lights a fourth candle)
And Dominique, my darling baby whom I loved more
than anyone. I used to tell you all my secrets, even
though you didn't understand them.
(lights the fifth candle)
Nathalie, you were not nice to me. You always tried to
steal Mama. And would pinch me, and then put your
hand on my mouth so no one could hear my screams.
But now I see I was not kind to you. You lost your
Mama and now I understand how that feels. You
needed to share Mama with me. Forgive me, my
cousin.
(lights the sixth candle)
And Joseph, your voice was just beginning to break
and we made such fun of you, and you hated that, you
were a shy boy, a sweet shy boy.

(lights the seventh candle)
And Jean-Pierre, the brilliant one. "The professor,"
Papa called you.
(lights the eighth candle)
And Solange, who loved all animals, so much, and
who had such a tender heart.
(lights the ninth candle)
And Marcel, the good-looking one, who Mama always
found excuses for if he did something bad.
(lights the tenth candle)
And Claude, who made Dominique give him her
sweets by frightening her with chameleons which she
hated.

Scene 14

Simon's office at the Refugee Centre.
Simon is totally absorbed in the pages Juliette has
brought him, She watches him intently, mirroring his
occasional smiles. Finally he looks up.

Simon   These descriptions are wonderful! You're a
          natural storyteller Juliette. It's marvellous. Where did
          Claude find chameleons?

Juliette   In the garden. He used to find one and
          pick it up with a stick and it would hold on to it, really
          tight, like this, you couldn't take it off and he would
          wave it under Dominique's nose, so she screamed.

Simon   And they really change colours all the
          time?

Juliette   My God any different colour, they are
          amazing Simon. If it's here it would look like this and
          if it's over there, like that. And sometimes many
          colours. If it was in the part of the garden where we

had many butterflies, with all different colours, it would be just like them, three colours or five.

Simon   Incredible!

Juliette   I know. They are beautiful but very scary.

Simon   Wow... It's these sort of wonderful details we want to get in your book. Have you got any more stories like these?

Juliette   Oh many, many.

Simon   Well then! And you must write about your grandparents too. That's a good way to bring in some of the history. Specially about the grandfather you told me was killed. You said that was when it all started – two generations ago.

Juliette   After the Independence.

Simon   In 1962.

Juliette   You know a lot, Simon.

Simon   Yes, well, I know a bit more, now, than I did.

Scene 15
Simon's office at the Refugee Centre.

Simon   Look, it's OK.

Juliette   Sorry, Simon.

Simon   No need to be, honestly, I know it's not easy. And I've still got quite a lot to type up, so I'll catch up with that, and then perhaps by next week, you'll have something.

Juliette   I think maybe I won't have time no more Simon, to come here every week.

Simon   What do you mean?

Juliette   I can only come maybe sometimes.

Simon   I don't understand. I... Can I ask why?

Juliette   I need to... I need to do things, Simon. I can't only do writing. Is no good. I need to start my life, get a job maybe, so I can get a place...

Simon   But you've got a place.

Juliette   It's a room, in a hostel.

Simon   OK, you can't stay there forever, but it's all right for now while you're finishing your book. *(smiles) You've* got a room at least, to write in! I've only got a shed! *(beat)* I thought your book was important to you.

Juliette   It is, but maybe I can finish it later.

Simon   No way, Juliette! Sorry, I didn't mean it like that. It's just that I really think you should keep going.

Juliette   It's too hard.

Simon   I know. But you must!

Juliette   Who are you Simon! Your book is in a drawer! So how you can say to me this?

Simon   *My* book! What's that's got to do with it! Anyway that's quite different.

Juliette   Why?

Simon   Because... I'm writing a completely different sort of book.

Juliette   Thank you! You don't write about your family! So why it is difficult for you? Why you cannot finish it? My book is too hard for me to finish, but you are writing just a storybook and you cannot do it. So how you want *me* to! Simon, you don't understand. I need to start my life, I need to live now, but every time I write, I'm there, I'm there! I don't want that no more. I want to be here! *(beat)* So, why is difficult for you, to finish your book?

Simon   Well, it's just... difficult.

Juliette   What is it about?

Simon   You really want to know?

Juliette   I do.

Simon   Well.... Well, maybe I'll tell you one day. It's your book that's important now.

Juliette   So, if your book is not important, why you are writing it?

Simon   Well, of course it's important to me. But you don't want to hear about it.

Juliette   It's too hard for me then, to understand?

Simon   No, no not at all, of course not. It's just, I didn't want to take up your time.

Juliette gives him a challenging look.

Simon   OK, well, basically, it's about a man... a man struggling to find himself, his identity. He's in this state of utter despair and he spends hours pouring it out to a psycho-analyst. But he begins to despise himself for being so self-obsessed, so caught up with his own ego, so he tries to counter this by writing a novel in which the 'I' ceases to exist, literally, there are no 'i's in the novel – the letter 'i' has been expunged. At the end you realise the book you are reading, which consists of his monologues to his therapist, in real time, is in fact, his novel. It's supposed to be a parody on urban western civilisation, the post-freudian cult of the individual, our obsessions with self, the fragmentation of modern life, our loss of continuity, of identity. *(beat)* It's supposed to be funny. And serious at the same time.

Juliette   So, why you cannot finish it?

Simon   It's very difficult, writing a book without any 'i's in it?

Juliette   Without eyes?

Simon   Well you can imagine. I can't use a word like difficult for example – that's got two 'i's, I have to find an alternative, like... 'hard'.

Juliette   Your book is too clever.

Simon   You think? Well, your book is too import-ant, too important to put in a drawer.
(*They both smile.*)
Right?

Scene 16
Simon's Office at the Refugee Centre.

Juliette   I'm so happy!

Simon   What? What's going on? What's happened? You haven't finished your book?

Juliette   No, it's my little brother, they found him in Uganda. Claude is alive!

Simon   My God, that's fantastic!

Juliette   I want to bring him here. Then I will have a family. I will look after him. Send him to school.

Simon   Well, that would be wonderful.

Juliette   He can go to university, be a doctor like Papa and we will have a new life in this country - together!

Simon   So, no writing today I take it?

Juliette   Oh yes. Letters. Please help me to write good letters.

Simon (*To audience*) Malcolm Wainright. The Entry Clearance Officer, British Embassy, Kampala, Uganda. Dear Mr Wainright, Re: Claude Gakwaya. I am writing to apply for entry clearance for the above named, my brother, whom I have only recently

discovered to be alive. I came to England in
September 1998, to escape further threats to myself
from the Hutus who burned down my family house
during the genocide of 1994, after all my family were
killed. To my great joy, I have been informed that my
younger brother, who is now sixteen, survived and is
presently living in Kampala. I have struggled for a
long time to find a reason to go on living and the
belief that I can be re-united with the sole surviving
member of my family has finally given me something
to live for. I urge you to respond favourably to this
application for family reunion. Yours sincerely ....

Juliette   Juliette Nyirabeza!

Scene 17

Juliette's room.
Simon is standing awkwardly near the doorway.
Juliette is sitting slumped, looking sullen and
withdrawn.

Simon   What happened to you, Juliette? Why
didn't you phone me? Why didn't you answer any of
my messages.
(Silence)
I've been worried about you. It's not like you.
(Silence)
Are you ill? Can I get you anything?
(Silence)
Why have you stopped coming to see me? What about
your book? Don't you want to finish it?

Juliette   I don't care about the book no more.

Simon   You don't care!

Juliette   No.

Simon   But you've nearly finished it! *(Juliette shrugs)* Oh right. So that's it then. Simon dismissed. *(beat)* I've given a lot of time to that book you know. Or perhaps you don't know. I've spent hours on it after our sessions, editing it, typing it up, and encouraging you, helping you, believing in you, believing this is important. Your 'mission'. The most important thing in your life.

Juliette   People are important.

Simon   Right! And you made them come alive again through your writing! And now you're nearly there.

Juliette   I don't care!

Simon   Well you should! *(beat)* Oh, come on Juliette, this is not like you. I don't believe you.

Juliette   It's *my* book.

Simon   Fine.

Juliette *(beat)* What you want from me?

Simon   Nothing. I came to see if you're all right.

Juliette   That is all?

Simon   OK, I admit I'm also hurt. Maybe I've got no right to be. I mean what's my little hurt against yours. I can't compete with that, can I? Ever. And maybe it's crazy to expect you to trust me, to trust anyone ever again, or consider other people's feelings, or say thank you or please again, all those social niceties, they must seem trivial to you now, like phoning someone to say, sorry I can't make our appointment today, or thank you Simon for all the work you've put in to help me write my book, you've been great, a great help, a great support, a friend. I know that for someone like you, this sort of thing must be unimportant. I'm just there to be used when it suits you. Survivors' Law. If you're not in the mood to show up for your appointment — tough, let him suffer a bit. I mean, it's nothing against what you've had to go through!

Juliette   You didn't come here to find out about my brother?

Simon   Well, of course I want to know about your brother. But you didn't do me the courtesy of letting me know when he's coming.

Juliette   He's not coming. The Home Office refused him.

She holds out the letter from the Home Office which he takes and reads.

Simon *(incredulous)* Oh my God, I don't believe it! After what you've been through! Bastards! When did you get this?

Juliette   The day I was coming to see you.

Simon   Oh Juliette, I'm... I'm so, so sorry. You must have been devastated. How thin you've become... even thinner than you were before. Please forgive all those things I just said. I had no idea. You poor, poor girl... how terrible for you.

Juliette   *Arrête!*

Simon   OK.

Juliette   Nobody must feel sorry for me!

Simon   OK, OK. *(Pause)* Is there anything I can...? Sorry.
(Silence) Do you want me to go?
*(Silence)*Do you want to talk about the book?

Juliette   No!

Simon   Do you want to talk about your brother?
(Pause) He was ten when... when you last saw him.

Juliette   He was ten when it happened.

Simon   Yes.

Juliette   Claude, he was the one who answered the door, when they came. They came to our house in the morning with our neighbour. This man, I used to play with his children. You can't imagine how I used to love his children. You know in Africa, people, they love each other. I used to do this for them, you know...? (*mimes plaiting of hair*)

Simon   Plaiting? Plaiting their hair?

Juliette   Yes. They lived just opposite, we used to go to each other's houses. He was just like a family friend, he was close to us. We used to invite him when we had a party, we did lots of things together. But it was he who brought the killers to our house. He didn't do the killing himself; he brought these men and said, "I think you should kill them." He gave the orders to the *interahamwe*. He wasn't a soldier, he was a civilian like my father, he was a businessman, he sold furniture. Then they told us, "Don't move, don't do anything, stay there." My mother said to us, "Now, please pray, pray, pray." They asked my father how he wanted to die. They told him if he wanted to die with a bullet, he would have to pay money, otherwise they would cut off his hands and then his arms and then his legs, take off everything slowly. My father begged them to take everything and leave. He gave them money but they asked for more. They asked for the rest of his money. My father went to his safe. As he was showing them the safe, one of the soldiers cut off his leg from behind. My father fell. While he was screaming they cut his throat and then sprayed him with bullets. My little sister Dominique was near my father and one of the bullets killed her. Then they cut my brother above the ear with a blade. He fell down. Then they said it will take too long, "Look, look the place is crawling with these Tutsi cockroaches." They used their pistols and they shot all my uncles and my other brothers. Then they said to me and my cousin and my older sister and my mother, "You come with us in our car". And then they took us where there is other women. *(Pause)* We survived too much, me and my mother and sisters and then finally they said, 'Now you must go with us to another place.' We were about forty women and they shot us one by one, by the side of a big pit. Only me, I was alive, the bullet didn't hit me. I was just lying there with the dead bodies around me, the blood running into my nose and my ears. I was the only one alive. I tried to climb out but I kept falling down. I tried for hours. Then I did it. It was night time now and I escaped into the forest. I will never forget this. Never. This is what happened to me and my family.

Scene 18

Simon   That night when I got back, I needed to talk. I said to Maggie, "Look, I've got something to tell you... it's pretty awful but I've just got to say it, get it off my chest." And she just said, "I know. I found the poems." Then she let rip, went mad − she'd sensed something for a while, but when she found 'my new love poems' as she called them, she'd realised. "I subsidise you to write because I make the mistake of thinking you're gifted and deserve a break and you have it off with one of your writing protégés." As crass as that. Horrendous. And then she laid in to me about the novel, which she'd also read. "Pretentious post-modern drivel!" she called it. "A waste of trees." "I know that," I yelled − we were both full at it by now. Then I found myself screaming Juliette's story at her − hysterical − we both were. "How dare she..." I said, "How could she even imagine that I'd actually...

with a young woman who'd been though... they're just... poems. My first poems for five years. My breakthrough." I slept on the sofa that night. Tried to. At about two in the morning, Maggie came down. To continue the row I thought, God! But no. She couldn't sleep she said, she'd been thinking about Juliette and her brother, their terrible story, and she had a suggestion. An inspired one. I mean it meant goodbye to the gîte in Normandy for the summer, but what the hell. "And by the way," she said. "The poems, they're good."

Juliette   Dear Simon, the smell of Africa is all around me now as I write you this letter. I was very fearful on the airplane, so nervous about coming back to Africa. My brother, I find him on the second day. I can't describe you how it was, like a miracle, we was so joyful. He is very big now, tall like our father. I have a bad shock when I see him because he has a very terrible scar on his face where they cut him with machete. His life has been very bad, even here in Uganda. He has been living in the streets. But now he is with good people, Jehovah's Witness. He works for them and they are helping him. We spend all the time together. We cry a lot but also we laugh sometimes. I want that he goes to university. I will send him money if I can to help him. Maybe he will go to Canada – if they take him. So then maybe I will try to go there. The most important thing for me is that he is alive. Now I want to finish my book very soon, so when I come back to London I will try to finish it with your help. Thank you for everything you do for me Simon, and thank you a million times for sending me to Uganda. You are like father to me, really. Kisses from Juliette.

Scene 19

A conference hall.
A conference podium. Simon and Juliette are waiting for their turn to do their presentations, both holding their prepared speeches in their hand. Juliette's is a single page and Simon's a number of pages. They speak straight out to the audience.

Simon   They've asked me to speak at this conference: 'Literature and Social Exclusion'. Something
the Arts Council set up. They want me to talk about
my work at the Refugee Centre, particularly about
Juliette. They wanted her to speak too, but she didn't
want to, said she couldn't. Her English, she said. But
then we drafted something together. Got it pretty
polished by the end. *And* she remembered to bring it
with her. Didn't leave it on the bus. Amazing how
quickly she finished it, once she got back from
Uganda. Something seemed to have shifted after that.
Seeing him alive and well.

Juliette   The English are strange people. I know
Simon a year now but he has never invited me to his
house. Africans would never be like this. One African
friend says the British like everything in a pigeon-
hole. What is that, I say. A pigeon-hole is like a
category. Here everything and everybody belongs in a
category. So if you are one thing to someone, like I am
a client to Simon at the Refugee Centre, you cannot
also be a friend because you cannot live in two
pigeon-holes at the same time.

Simon *(taking up his position at the microphone,*
addressing conference audience) What I'd like to talk
about today is the power of writing. I started working

with refugees wanting to write out their stories just over a year ago and the very first person I met at the Centre when I started, was a young lady from Rwanda...

Juliette   Soon it will be my turn. I'm so nervous I don't think any sound will come from my mouth when I have to do my speech. A man is introducing us and he just said my name so I wanted to disappear. Disappear.

Simon (*finishing his talk*) Finally, I would just like to say that it has been a privilege for me to work with Juliette on her book. And now I'd like to hand you over to Juliette, who will say a few words. Juliette?

Juliette remains rooted to the spot, the paper with her speech written on it clutched in her hand. She steps forward and after what seems like an interminable pause, starts to read stiffly from the paper.

Juliette   Ladies and gentlemen. I have documented, *doc*-umented in my book, not only the horr... horrendious... horrendous atrocities perpe*trate*d against ...

Juliette suddenly breaks off, choked with emotion. A long awkward silence ensues, as she struggles to re-find her voice. When she does it starts shaky and then builds. The paper with her prepared speech is now abandoned and gets more and more crumpled in her hand as she finds her own voice.

My book.... is the story of what happened to me and my people. It was very hard to write, very painful, but now I have finished it, I feel clean. *(looks at Simon)* I can sleep. I can eat. I can walk in the park. I can see the flowers, see the sky.

I wrote my book to take the pain from my heart. But also I wrote this book to help all people in the world who feel hopeless, who think they have nothing to live for. When I finished to write this book, two things happened to me: my terrible headaches and my nightmares which I had for five years stopped and I found an answer to the question: Does life have a meaning? That was a question I asked myself all the time because if it has a meaning, why has all this happened? And now I think I have found the answer, through writing this book. So please when it is published I ask you to read it so that what happened can go a bit into your hearts and away from ours and so the people who were killed will not be forgotten.

She stops abruptly and looks at Simon who signals to her. They both read from the text of her manuscript.

Simon   "Once upon a time..."
Juliette   *Chera... ***
   [Kera]
Simon   "... in the heart of Africa..."
Juliette   *... umutima wa africa...**
   [umutima w' Africa]
Simon   "... there was a small paradise, a beautiful country of forests and lakes and mountains..."
Juliette   *... harijihoogoo chamatanawbootchi ijihoogoo ...**
   [hari igihugu cy'amata n'ubucyi]
Simon   "...which we called the land of milk and honey... "

Juliette   *... chimisawzi ijihumbi...**
[cy imisozi]
"and the country of a thousand hills."

The End.